The Woman God Built

The Woman God Built: Obedience Looks Good on Me

Donniseca West

Ink'd by Heaven™

Copyright

Published by Ink'd by Heaven™

ISBN: 979-8-9940723-9-4 (Paperback)

Revised & Expanded Edition

Printed in the United States of America

Dedication

This book is dedicated to the woman I was when obedience felt lonely,
when healing felt slow, and when choosing God meant letting go of everything familiar.

To my husband—
for standing with me through becoming, not perfection.

To my children—
for watching me become before I ever taught.

And to every woman who has whispered,
"God, is this really what You have for me?"

Yes.
And more.

Acknowledgments

First and always, I acknowledge God.
Not as a concept, but as the Architect of every chapter in my life.
This book exists because He stayed when others left, spoke when I was silent, and built what I could not. Every word here is evidence of His patience, mercy, and insistence on my becoming.

To the seasons that stretched me—thank you.
The silence, the waiting, the breaking, and the rebuilding were not wasted. Each one refined my voice, strengthened my discernment, and anchored my obedience.

To my family—thank you for your grace.
For loving me through growth. For giving me space to become. For allowing me to choose healing and purpose even when it required change.

To the women who trusted me with their stories, questions, and becoming—this book carries you with it. You sharpened my calling, confirmed my assignment, and reminded me why obedience matters.

To the Becoming Her Council™—you are living proof that healing is not theoretical. You embody the work, the courage, and the faith this book stands for.

And to the woman reading this:
Thank you for saying yes to yourself.
Thank you for staying open.
Thank you for becoming.

This book is part of what God is building—but it is not the end.
It is an invitation.

Foreword

God, Are You Listening?

There were nights I didn't pray—I just cried.

I didn't have the words. I didn't have the strength.
I had a whisper in my spirit and tears on my pillow.
And in those moments, I found myself asking:

God... are You listening?

I didn't want another sermon.
I wasn't looking for pretty quotes or polished advice.
I needed a move.

I needed to know that the God I believed in could reach into my real life—
into my heartbreak,
my health crises,
my kitchen floor at 3 a.m.—
and show up.

And He did.

Not always in the way I expected.
But always in the way I needed.

This book is the story of a woman who wasn't supposed to make it.
A woman who was counted out, overlooked,

underestimated—
yet chose obedience anyway.

I chose healing.
I chose truth.
I chose joy.

And in that choosing, I discovered God moving in every chapter of my life.

If you've ever felt invisible, forgotten, stuck, or simply tired—
I wrote this for you.

Every chapter holds a piece of my journey.
Every truth was paid for with tears and tenacity.
And every word stands as a reminder that you are not weak, not dramatic, and not alone.

This is not just a memoir.
It is a mirror.

Because while you're reading my story,
you may find yourself recognizing your own.

He is listening.
You have been heard.
And now—it's your time.

With love and raw truth,

Donniseca West

Table of Contents

Contents

Chapter 1: Valedictorian with a Vision

In the spring of 1997, I stood beneath the open sky on my high school's football field in Chicago, navy gown billowing and gold sash pressed proudly across my chest. I was Valedictorian—number one in my class—and my name rang through the loudspeaker like a victory cry. I had earned this. Every sleepless night, every study group, every prayer whispered into a tear-stained pillow led to this moment. I was Donniseca Dillon back then—and I was unstoppable.

The sun was warm on my back as I stepped up to the mic. I remember glancing at the crowd, feeling equal parts powerful and petrified. But as soon as I opened my mouth, the words flowed with grace and grit. My future felt wide open, paved in purpose and possibility.

I had just ended my toxic off-and-on relationship with Donovan, the high school sweetheart who had broken my heart more times than I could count. For the first time in years, I was single, soaring, and truly free. My face card was undefeated, my waistline was snatched, and my dreams were high-rise level. I was college-bound and determined to rewrite my family's story through the pages of my own success.

The first semester of college was everything I hoped it would be. I breezed through classes, balanced a part-time job, and felt like I was finally becoming the woman God had always intended. Education was more than a goal for me—it was a lifeline. It was my escape from generational struggle and silence.

But when winter break arrived, so did the storm.

One morning, in our small kitchen on the South Side, my mother Kari stirred a pot of Cream of Wheat like it was the only thing she could control. The heater hissed behind us, fighting to warm the cold that seemed to live in our walls.

She wouldn't look at me when she said it.

"I can't give you any more money for school."

The words hit like bricks. Not because I was surprised—deep down I had sensed the distance—but because I had hoped she'd fight for my future the way I was. She could've helped more. She just chose not to. Education never meant to her what it meant to me. For her, survival was enough. For me, school was survival.

I had pieced together scholarships, financial aid, and paychecks, but it still wasn't enough. After exhausting every option and every tear, I packed my things. College didn't expel me. Poverty did.

I moved back to Chicago and in with my best friend Paisley, who had a steady boyfriend and a two-bedroom apartment that smelled like cocoa butter and ambition. We were 19, reckless with hope, and still believed life could be figured out one Friday night at a time.

Through her boyfriend, I met Micah.

Tall. Charismatic. Dangerous in the way only charming men with no real plans can be. He wore confidence like cologne, and it filled every room he walked into. At first, it felt like fate. We clicked fast and deep. Before long, we were "a thing."

What I thought was love was really trauma bonding in designer packaging.

Micah and I got engaged—twice. We even applied for two marriage licenses. But both times, something deep inside me froze. A voice I couldn't name whispered "don't do it. I tried to silence it, tried to convince myself I was just scared of commitment. But I wasn't. I was scared of repeating my mother's story.

We bounced around apartments, playing house in chaos. I had no blueprint for stability—just the determination to create something better for myself. I was tired, emotionally drained, and spiritually empty.

And then one night, everything went black.

I collapsed in a cold sweat. My body felt like it was fighting against me. I was rushed to the hospital, drifting in and out of consciousness, tubes and monitors attached to every limb.

Diabetic Ketoacidosis. DKA. My blood sugar was so high my body had begun to poison itself.

The doctors were whispering. Nurses moving fast. Then came the moment that would change my life.

"Miss Dillon," the nurse said gently, "You're four months pregnant."

I couldn't breathe. I was four months pregnant—and had no idea.

In the middle of crisis, God whispered life.

When Ariyah was born, the world shifted. She was stunning. Her eyes searched mine like she already knew who I was. In her, I found purpose. She was softness in a world that had hardened me.

But two weeks after bringing her home, the betrayal that would break me hit like a freight train.

Paisley—my best friend, my ride-or-die—confessed that she had slept with Micah.

I stood there in our shared kitchen, my baby in my arms and silence between us like a wall. My knees threatened to give out. My soul cracked.

Sometimes betrayal doesn't come with warning signs. Sometimes it comes dressed as love.

I forgave them both. Not because they deserved it—but because I refused to carry rage while raising a queen.

Micah and I tried to salvage what was left. But he wouldn't work. He cheated like it was a sport. Lied like it was scripture. By 22, I was done.

That breakup was more than the end of a relationship. It was the beginning of me. Not the pretty version. The real one. The broken, rising, healing one.

I didn't know it then, but that was the moment I began my journey of becoming whole—the woman who would one day lead others out of the same darkness I had to crawl through.

Because sometimes the greatest act of love...

is walking away with your head high and your name still intact.

Reflection

Scripture: Habakkuk 2:3 (NIV)

"For the revelation awaits an appointed time; it speaks of the end and will not prove false.

Though it linger, wait for it; it will certainly come and will not delay."

I had the grades. The vision. The grit. But what do you do when life slams the door in your face just as you're about to walk through it? You don't fold. You don't break. You pivot and rise.

God doesn't cancel vision—He cultivates it in hidden places. That closed door at college wasn't the end. It was the reroute. The detour to destiny.

Just because you find yourself back home doesn't mean you're starting over. Sometimes the delay is divine. Sometimes being "sent back" is actually being set up.

My worth is not wrapped in degrees or diplomas. It's wrapped in the fact that God already saw me whole—even when I was collapsing from the weight of it all.

Affirmation

"I am not defined by detours. What looked like a setback was actually a setup. I am walking in God's timing, God's covering, and God's vision for my life. My pain will have purpose. I may have been delayed—but I am not denied."

Sacred Prompts

When was the first time you felt your dream slip through your fingers?

Write about what happened and how you processed it.

Have you ever felt unsupported by someone you depended on?

What did it teach you about trust, boundaries, and emotional independence?

What “delays” in your life might actually be divine redirections?

Ask God to show you the lesson in the detour.

What parts of your story still carry shame?

How can you begin to rewrite the narrative with grace and power?

Chapter 2: Becoming the Woman Who Leaves

"There's a moment every woman reaches—not when she's tired of him, but when she's ready for her."

After I left Micah, everything felt like both an ending and a beginning. I didn't have a clear plan, but I had Ariyah, and I had peace—and that was enough to start.

I remember the first morning we woke up alone. Just me and my daughter in a studio apartment with more dreams than furniture. The space was small, but it was ours. I boiled water for oatmeal on a borrowed hot plate, humming gospel under my breath while Ariyah giggled in her bassinet. There was still grief. Still heartbreak. But for the first time in a long time, I could hear myself Think. And what I heard was: You were never the problem. I stopped shrinking. I stopped waiting for Micah to be someone he never intended to become. And I started showing up for the woman I had abandoned: me.

There was no crowd cheering. No miracle moment. Just slow, daily decisions to love myself back to life. I enrolled in a certification program. Applied for every job I could find. I was still tired, still healing—but I was moving. And movement, even weary, is a declaration of life.

I started journaling again. Talking to God again. Looking in the mirror without wincing. My confidence came back in fragments—like puzzle pieces scattered across time—but each one fit tighter than before.

And the best part?

Ariyah watched it all.

She watched me cry in the bathroom and fix my face before walking out.

She watched me budget down to the last dollar and still tithe on faith. She watched me say “no” when the wrong man came knocking.

I wasn't just building a life—I was rebuilding legacy.

Leaving Micah wasn't the end of my story. It was the first time I picked up the pen and started writing my own.

And this time? I was the main character. Not the background support. Not the fixer. Not the survivor.

The woman.

The whole, healing, bold woman who finally believed she deserved more.

Reflection

— Isaiah 43:18–19 (ESV)

"Remember not the former things, nor consider the things of old. Behold, I am doing a new thing; now it springs forth, do you not perceive it?"

I didn't lose myself. I left myself behind—because survival demanded it. But then, God was calling me to return.

There is divine strength in a woman who chooses to stop surviving and start living. When you leave what broke you, heaven rejoices. Because choosing you isn't selfish. It's sacred. It's surrendering to God's plan instead of clinging to your own patterns.

Let Him rebuild you in the quiet, in the broken spaces. He specializes in holy renovations.

Affirmation

"I release what wounded me and return to what God called me to be. I am not broken—I am becoming."

Sacred Prompts

What parts of yourself did you silence or abandon during that relationship?

What daily habits can you begin today that honor your healing?

If your daughter or younger self watched your life right now, what would you want her to see?

Where is God calling you to move forward, even if you're still afraid?

Chapter 3: Building While Bleeding

"Some women break down after heartbreak. I built something instead."

By 22, I had two things I could truly call mine: my daughter Ariyah... and a broken heart patched together with survival instinct and silent prayers.

Devon was out of the picture—finally. No more tears, no more hoping he'd change. He left, and this time, I let the door hit him. That relationship drained me emotionally, wrecked me financially, and left my spirit threadbare. But even then, I couldn't stop. I had a baby girl watching my every move. I had to keep going.

The truth? I was used to doing life alone.

My mama, Kari, wasn't the type to rally around me when life got hard. She was quiet. Judgmental. Always looking like, she wanted to say something but never quite getting it out. Or worse—saying it with that sharp side-eye of disappointment that made you feel like you failed just by breathing too loud.

She didn't offer support, not really. She didn't guide. Didn't affirm. And while she didn't throw me away, she also didn't show up in any meaningful way either. She was there. But never really with me.

So, I learned to show up for myself.

I wiped my tears, threw my hair in a bun, and said, "God, if You'll lead, I'll follow."

And just like that, He gave me a next step.

I enrolled in school to become a Certified Medical Assistant. It wasn't glamorous. It didn't come with applause. But it was something I could build on. Something that said: You're not done yet.

I was balancing diapers, night feedings, and anatomy flashcards, but for the first time in a long time—I felt purpose again.

Graduation day was quiet. No balloons. No bouquet. Just me and Ariyah, riding the bus home with a rolled-up certificate and a Dollar Tree frame in a plastic bag. But I smiled the whole ride. Because I did it.

For her. For me.

I got a job running the front desk at a fast-paced, multi-doctor medical practice. Phones rang nonstop. Patients rolled in with attitudes and ailments. I managed schedules, answered three lines at once, fixed the copier when it jammed, and still made it to daycare pickup on time.

That job gave me rhythm. Routine. A paycheck that didn't bounce.

And then came the real shift...

At 25, I landed my first corporate job.

I'll never forget walking into that downtown office with my thrifted blazer, a cheap but cute handbag, and nerves tight in my stomach. That ID badge? Felt like a trophy. My desk had a nameplate. I had benefits. I had made it.

I was the first in my family to have a salaried position with health insurance and a 401(k). Nobody clapped. No one celebrated. But I knew what that moment meant.

It meant I didn't die in the valley.

It meant every sleepless night, every betrayal, every tear had led to something.

But even with that good job, even with my own desk and a steady check—I was lonely.

Not for company. Not for friends. I had people around me.

But I wanted presence. A person. A partner.

That's when Donovan came back.

Yep. That Donovan. The high school sweetheart who had me twisted in my teens. He slid back into my life like he never left. Said he was married—but separated. Claimed I was "the one that got away."

I should've paused. Should've prayed. But instead, I leaned into the fantasy. We started talking. Reconnecting. Laughing like no time had passed. It was sweet...until it wasn't.

He promised the divorce was coming. I believed him.

I even helped him file.

I helped him end something, thinking I was helping us begin.

Eventually, we got married. It felt like redemption. Like all the lonely nights had finally paid off.

But behind that marriage certificate?

Was a storm that would demand every ounce of strength I had left.

Reflection

Isaiah 61:3 (NKJV)

"To give them beauty for ashes, the oil of joy for mourning, the garment of praise for the spirit of heaviness..."

I was Built in the Bleeding Season

Nobody saw the war going on inside of me.

The tear-stained pillows. The doubt wrapped in ambition. The way you held your daughter in one hand and your broken dreams in the other.

I was building while bleeding.

Smiling at work while crying in silence. Earning degrees with an empty heart. Holding the world together while no one held me.

But God was watching. And what they didn't applaud—He anointed.

This chapter of my life may not have looked holy, but it was holy ground. Because even in disappointment, I didn't give up.

I pivoted.

I pressed on.

I put one foot in front of the other, even when my soul screamed to collapse.

And that job? That certificate? That breakthrough?

It wasn't just about income.

It was about identity—God showing me that my survival wasn't the end of my story.

It was the beginning of my legacy.

Affirmation

I am not broken—I am being rebuilt. Even in the dark, God is birthing something radiant within me. My labor is not in vain.

Sacred Prompts

What parts of you did you rebuild during your most painful seasons?

When have you felt God strengthening you behind the scenes, even when no one else noticed?

Have you ever mistaken loneliness for readiness in a relationship? What was the cost?

What would it look like to finally celebrate yourself, without waiting for applause?

What "beauty for ashes" moment has God given you that still makes you weep in gratitude?

Chapter 4: When the Storm Woke Me Up

"Rock bottom taught me more than peace ever could."

Marriage wasn't what I expected. Not even close.

I thought Donovan and I had finally gotten it right. We had the history, the spark, and now, the papers. But what we didn't have was healing—not his, not mine, and certainly not together.

He was moody. Unmotivated. Still dancing around the edges of the street life, blaming everyone but himself for where he was in life. I was doing it all—paying the bills, raising our daughter, carrying our son, working full-time, and managing my type 1 diabetes with the discipline of a soldier. But inside? I was quietly breaking.

When our son was born, I was 28. A second miracle in the middle of mayhem. I loved him deeply. But I was tired. So tired. Spiritually dry. Physically worn. Emotionally silenced.

And still, I believed if I just held on tighter, he would change. I kept hoping he'd rise up, get a job, be a father, show up for our family.

Instead, he cheated. And lied. And kept treating me like the enemy while I was carrying the entire war.

Then came the night that changed everything.

A fight exploded—loud, cruel, full of words you can't take back. He stormed out. And that night, my body surrendered.

I had a TIA—a mini-stroke. I woke up unable to feel the left side of my body. My babies were crying, and I couldn't move. I couldn't speak. I was paralyzed in more ways than one.

Paisley, my best friend, was the one who rushed to my side as the paramedics wheeled me away. Her face was full of fear, her voice trembling as she told me, "You can't die. Your kids need you. We need you."

And I knew... this wasn't just a wake-up call. It was my divine redirection.

But let me be honest—I didn't leave right away.

There were months after that stroke where I tried to make the marriage work. I begged him to come with me into something new. I told him we both needed to start over, to save what little was left. I pleaded for us to move forward together. I even begged him for a divorce when I saw he wasn't trying—but he refused. He acted like my pain was my problem, like my healing was my burden alone.

So, I prayed.

And then I planned.

I called my boss and asked if I could transfer to our Texas office. Within 48 hours, they said yes. I found an apartment online, mapped the route, and circled a moving date on my calendar with trembling hands.

When I told Donovan, he shrugged. "Do what you gotta do," he said. No protest. No tears. No intention of helping.

He didn't lift a single finger to help me move. He didn't pack a bag. He didn't check the tires on my car or see if I had enough gas money.

So, I loaded up my car with two babies, a trunk full of faith, and an insulin bag strapped to my side.

And I drove. From Chicago to Texas.

He let me go.

He let us go.

He let the only woman who ever stood beside him through prison, poverty, betrayal, and childbirth pack up and leave without looking back.

And as crazy as it sounds—that was the beginning of my freedom.

Reflection

Scripture: Psalm 18:6 (NKJV)

"In my distress I called upon the Lord, and cried out to my God; He heard my voice from His temple, and my cry came before Him, even to His ears."

Sometimes, your greatest breakthrough begins at your lowest point.

God doesn't always pull us out right away—sometimes He lets us collapse just enough to realize that what we were leaning on was never solid to begin with.

In my weakness, He was forming strength. In my silence, He was teaching me to hear Him. And in my storm, He was preparing my exodus.

The day I packed that car and drove into the unknown, I was walking in the spirit of Abraham—leaving my comfort zone, my people, and my mother's house for a land I had not yet seen...but believed in.

That's faith. And that's favor.

Affirmation

I am not lost. I am led. Even in my breaking, God is birthing something beautiful. I trust Him to make rivers in my wilderness.

Sacred Prompts

What did you have to leave in order to heal?

How did God provide for you when no one else showed up?

In what ways did hitting rock bottom reveal your true strength?

What parts of you are still healing from that transition?

What would you say to the version of you who was packing that car?

Chapter 5: The Doorstep and the Decision

"Sometimes closure doesn't come with a conversation. It comes with clarity."

It was hot. Texas hot. The kind of heat that sticks to your skin like your past trying to follow you.

I had just begun to settle into my new apartment. Ariyah was adjusting to a new school. My son was still in diapers. I was working hard, praying harder, and trying to breathe. Every breath felt like a reset—like I was inhaling the future and exhaling everything I'd survived.

I didn't think I'd see him again. Not after the way he let us go so easily. But about a month after I moved, Donovan showed up.

On my doorstep.

No call. No warning. Just... there. Standing with a duffel bag and those same empty eyes that once held promises.

I should've slammed the door. But closure is tricky when your heart is still bruised, and your mind still plays reruns of the life you thought you'd build together.

I let him in. Temporarily. Not into my heart—but into the space where pity and hope still danced.

He said all the right things: “I’m sorry.” “I’ve changed.” “Let’s try again.”

But words without fruit are just noise.

Within weeks, he was back to his old patterns. Sleeping in while I worked. Not helping with the kids. Avoiding responsibility. I was doing it all again—this time in a hotter state with a heavier heart.

And then came the breaking point.

I had started blacking out in my sleep. My blood sugar was crashing—fast and often. Stress and Type 1 Diabetes don’t mix. I would wake up on the floor, surrounded by paramedics, scared out of my mind.

But the worst moment?

One morning, I heard Ariyah crying. My daughter. My little girl who had already seen too much.

“Mommy! Wake up! Please wake up!”

I could hear her. I just couldn’t respond.

My body was failing. And this man—this husband—was sleeping through the alarm of my life falling apart.

I begged him again to help. To step up. To get a job. To make a plan so I could at least co-parent in peace.

He refused.

Instead, he stole every penny I had. Drained my bank account. Left it over drafted.

And then, in the middle of the night, he left.

No goodbye. No note. Just gone.

I should’ve been angry.

But I wasn’t.

I was free.

I was finally free.

Reflection

Scripture: Psalm 34:17-18 (NLT)

"The Lord hears his people when they call to him for help. He rescues them from all their troubles. The Lord is close to the brokenhearted; he rescues those whose spirits are crushed."

Sometimes your deliverance doesn't come with celebration—it comes in silence. In the midnight hour. In the form of someone walking out who was never meant to stay.

I didn't lose a covering. I lost a burden.

I didn't get abandoned. I got released.

God allowed him to leave so that I could live. Sometimes the greatest act of love God shows us is by removing what we won't let go of.

Affirmation

I am not abandoned—I am chosen. God's plan for me includes freedom, healing, and protection. Even in heartbreak, I am held.

Sacred Prompts

What pain did you mistake for love in this season?

What are the warning signs you ignored?

How did God show up for you in the silence?

What changed the moment you realized he was gone for good?

In what ways did that midnight exit mark the beginning of your becoming?

Chapter 6: The Real Me Moved to Texas

"Sometimes the most powerful version of you is born the moment you choose yourself."

Freedom didn't feel like fireworks or fanfare—it felt like quiet. Like waking up without panic. Like checking my bank account and not seeing it emptied by someone I trusted. It felt like not waiting for the sound of footsteps or slammed doors or the anxiety of wondering who I needed to be that day just to keep the peace.

After Donovan left, I didn't fall apart.

I rose.

Not quickly. Not loudly. But faithfully.

Texas wasn't just a move. It was a reset. A divine rerouting. God didn't just remove me from a bad situation—He positioned me for restoration. The apartment was simple, the furniture was minimal, but there was peace in every corner. And peace, for me, was a luxury I had learned to live without for far too long.

The days were full—early mornings, long hours, lunch breaks spent praying, evenings spent cuddling my babies, and late nights spent journaling with worship music humming in the background.

But this time, I wasn't surviving.

I was healing.

I wasn't searching for love—I was learning to love me. I wasn't chasing validation—I was claiming identity. I woke up every day asking God, "Who am I without the chaos?" And day by day, He showed me.

I began doing things just for me. Taking walks. Buying a new lipstick shade. Reorganizing my closet to reflect the woman I was becoming, not the girl who had settled. I looked in the mirror and, for the first time in a long time, I didn't flinch. I smiled.

I started to dance again—sometimes with my daughter, sometimes in the kitchen alone while dinner simmered on the stove and worship filled the room.

That summer, I became a mother who wasn't afraid of her own Sacred.

I became the kind of woman who taught her children joy not by telling them—but by living it.

It wasn't perfect.

I was still tired.

I was still learning how to manage my diabetes more intentionally, how to budget down to the penny, and how to release the shame I didn't even realize I was carrying.

But I was free. Not just from a man—but from a mindset.

Texas didn't heal me.

God did.

But He used that space, that season, that silence to do it.

And in that silence, the real me emerged—not the one defined by heartbreak, motherhood, or survival... but the one defined by grace, grit, and growth.

Reflection

Scripture: Psalm 23:3 (ESV)

"He restores my soul. He leads me in paths of righteousness for His name's sake."

There's a moment in every woman's life where she has to look in the mirror and ask, "Who am I without the trauma? Without the mask? Without the need to perform for love?" That's the moment healing begins.

Texas wasn't a vacation—it was holy ground. Because healing doesn't always happen in a hospital or a therapy office. Sometimes it happens between loads of laundry. In whispered prayers over dinner. In a quiet kitchen where the chaos is finally gone and all that's left is you—and God.

Beloved, God didn't need my perfection to restore me. He needed my *yes*. My surrender. My stillness.

The real me was not too much, too broken, or too far gone. She was simply waiting for permission to breathe again.

And guess what? I just gave it to her.

Affirmation

- I am worthy of peace, love, and restoration.
- I honor the woman I am becoming—present, powerful, and full of purpose.
- I am no longer surviving. I am healing, whole, and held by God.

Sacred Prompts:

1. In what ways have you begun to rediscover yourself after loss or heartbreak?
2. What daily routines or quiet moments bring you peace?
3. What are you ready to release so you can experience true restoration?

Chapter 7: When Strength Looks Like Softness

"I didn't lose myself—I laid her down to rest so I could rise stronger."

The fall after my healing summer wasn't loud. It didn't come crashing in with bold announcements or big moments. It came gently—like the way God speaks when you finally get quiet enough to hear Him.

I was working my job, taking care of my kids, living a life that looked normal from the outside—but inside, something deeper was taking root. I had tasted peace, and now I was craving more of it. More wholeness. More alignment. More God.

My prayer life deepened. I stopped performing for people and started showing up for myself. I began saying no without guilt. I rested without apology. And that—that—was new.

Before, I wore strength like armor. I was the fixer, the strong friend, the one who made things happen even if it cost me everything. But now? I started realizing that strength could look like softness, too. It could look like boundaries. Like tears. Like vulnerability. Like taking the cape off and saying, "God, I need You."

I wasn't rushing anymore. I wasn't desperate. I was learning to be content without being complacent. That season taught me that healing doesn't always shout. Sometimes it just shows up in how you speak to yourself.

One night, I sat on my balcony, sipping tea, journaling by candlelight while the kids slept. The Texas air was warm, and my heart was finally still. And I heard God whisper: "You're ready."

Ready for what? I didn't know. But I trusted Him. Because He had brought me this far. And for the first time in a long time—I wasn't afraid of what was next.

I was starting to feel like a woman again. Not just a mother. Not just a worker. But a whole, vibrant, beautiful woman.

And that woman? She was worth the wait.

Reflection

Scripture: Psalm 46:10 (NIV)

"Be still, and know that I am God."

My stillness was not a setback—it was sacred. In the quiet moments, God rebuilt my identity. He reminded me that strength isn't always about striving. Sometimes, it's about surrender.

Let yourself soften. There is power in peace.

Affirmation

I am strong enough to rest, wise enough to wait, and whole enough to honor my softness. I am becoming everything God intended, in His timing.

Sacred Prompts

When did you begin to see softness as strength?

What boundaries did you create to protect your peace?

How did your relationship with God shift during this season?

In what moments did you begin to feel whole again?

Who are you becoming—and what does she need from you today?

Chapter 8: A Divine Interruption

"Sometimes your greatest awakening comes wrapped in a divine connection."

Life had finally started to feel steady. I was holding it all together—my job, my babies, my peace. I wasn't dating. I wasn't searching. I was simply flowing. Focused on God, focused on me. Focused on being present for my kids.

That summer, something shifted in me. I prayed deeper, laughed louder, and reintroduced myself to the woman I was proud to become. I wasn't chasing healing—I was walking in it.

Then came the moment that would change everything.

One night, out of pure curiosity and maybe a little boredom, I created an online dating profile. I had no real expectations. I just wanted to see what was out there now that I knew who I was. I had standards. Boundaries. Peace I wasn't willing to trade for company.

But then... I saw him.

His profile wasn't like the others. It had depth. Heart. His smile was warm, and his eyes told a story. Something in my spirit stirred, and I sent him a personal message.

He responded. We chatted online for a few minutes, and then he sent his number.

Our first phone call lasted for hours.

That first week, we talked like old friends. A week later, we went on our first date. When I saw him for the first time, I knew. I knew. But I didn't trust myself—at least not yet. I had chosen wrong before, so I tried to slow it down... even end it. But God had other plans.

We met in September 2012. By February 2013, we were married.

His name is Jason.

He was more than I ever prayed for. He was made for me—and me for him. Recently divorced himself, he understood my story, my strength, my softness. He didn't try to fix me. He covered me.

This wasn't lust. It wasn't fantasy. This was legacy.

Reflection

Scripture: Proverbs 18:22 (NIV)

"He who finds a wife finds what is good and receives favor from the Lord."

I didn't have to chase love when I was walking with the Author of it. When God is the matchmaker, the connection comes with peace, not confusion.

Let this chapter remind you: You are still worthy of a love that honors you.

Affirmation

I am seen, chosen, and loved by a man who reflects God's heart. I didn't settle—I was settled into.

Sacred Prompts

How did your healing prepare you for love?

What did you learn about yourself before meeting your partner?

How did your relationship confirm what God had been preparing you for?

In what ways did your husband show up differently from anyone else?

What would you say to the woman who's given up on love?

Chapter 9: Becoming Whole Wasn't Instant

"Wholeness isn't a finish line—it's a rhythm of grace, rest, and becoming."

Marrying Jason wasn't the end of the story—it was the beginning of a new one. For the first time in my adult life, I felt safe. Safe to breathe. Safe to bloom. Safe to believe that I didn't have to fight for love anymore.

But here's the truth nobody talks about; even when love is good, healing still has to happen. Just because you're no longer in survival mode doesn't mean the wounds vanish. They just get quiet until something touches them again.

Jason was patient, but I had trust issues. I still braced for the worst when everything was good. I'd watch him sleep and wonder if it would all be taken from me. It wasn't about him—it was about the broken pieces of me that were still learning what peace felt like.

I had to learn how to receive—without apology. Love. Help. Rest. Grace.

I had been in control for so long that softness felt like weakness. But Jason didn't require me to be strong every second. He covered me. He prayed over me. He didn't fix everything—but he stayed present.

And that was new for me.

We were blending lives—two whole adults with pasts, kids, expectations, and dreams. And even though I had found the one, I still had to find me again within this new chapter.

I had to rediscover what brought me joy—not just as a wife or mother, but as Donniseca.

I started writing again. Creating. Pouring into other women who had been through fire and were still standing. That's when the vision for Wife Builders started brewing in my spirit. A space where women could be honest, healed, and holy—without having to choose between being soft and being strong.

Becoming whole wasn't instant. It was layered, messy, and holy. But I kept showing up.

For me.

For my marriage.

For the woman I was always becoming.

Reflection

Scripture – 1 Peter 5:10 (ESV)

"And after you have suffered a little while, the God of all grace... will himself restore, confirm, strengthen, and establish you."

Healing doesn't end with the wedding. Sometimes it starts after the promise. God uses the safety of love to reveal the places that still need tending. Let Him restore the parts of you that survival had to silence.

Affirmation

I am healing in the safety of love. I am allowed to be both soft and strong, both chosen and becoming.

Sacred Prompts

What surprised you most about your healing journey after marriage?

In what ways did God use your partner to reflect His love for you?

What parts of your identity were rediscovered in your new chapter?

How did you learn to trust again—yourself, your partner, and God?

What does wholeness mean to you now?

Chapter 10: The Woman I Prayed to Become

"Sometimes you don't even recognize her at first—but when you do, you realize you are the woman you prayed to become."

I used to think becoming whole meant arriving somewhere polished—no cracks, no struggle, no trace of the girl who used to cry on the bathroom floor.

But here's what I know now: God doesn't erase her. He builds on her. He resurrects her.

By the time I hit my mid-thirties, I could look back and see the thread. From the tear-stained dorm room to the cramped Chicago apartment. From the delivery room to the courtroom. From over drafted bank accounts to the front seat of favor. It had all been working—every ache, every delay, every betrayal—was setting me up to become her.

I no longer questioned whether I was enough. I knew I was. I had survived the death of a dream, the destruction of a marriage, the sting of betrayal, and the lies I once told myself just to cope. And still—I rose. Not in bitterness, but in brilliance.

Jason and I weren't just surviving—we were thriving. Not because we had it all figured out, but because we had surrendered the script and let God write something better.

My children were growing up strong. I was building a life I didn't need to recover from. And my heart? It finally felt safe in its own chest.

There's a kind of peace that doesn't make noise. It just sits with you in the morning while you sip coffee, or hums in your spirit as you fold laundry and thank God for the silence after the storm.

And that's where I found her—the woman I prayed to become. She didn't look like the magazine version. She wasn't perfect. But she was whole.

She was rooted.

She was finally home in her own skin.

And best of all?

She wasn't done becoming.

Reflection

Scripture – Philippians 1:6 (NLT)

"And I am certain that God, who began the good work within you, will continue his work until it is finally finished on the day when Christ Jesus returns."

I was still becoming. There's no shame in that. This is not my finish line—it's was a sacred milestone. So, Don't rush your healing. Don't belittle your progress. God is not finished with you yet—and that's good news.

Affirmation

I am the answered prayer of the woman I used to be. I honor my journey, I embrace my healing, and I trust the process of becoming.

Sacred Prompts

In what ways have you already become the woman you once prayed for?

What remnants of your past are you learning to honor instead of resent?

How has peace shown up in your life without making noise?

What do you want your "next level" of becoming to look like?

Who are you committed to becoming for the rest of your story?

Chapter 11: The Birth of Wife Builders — Becoming Her First

"Wife Builders was never about building marriages. It was about forming women who are whole enough to steward whatever God entrusts to them."

Wife Builders did not begin with marriage.

It began with *becoming*.

Before there was a platform, a program, or a community, there was a woman in formation—being stripped of performance, healed of survival, and invited into alignment. God was not rushing me toward outcomes. He was rooting me in identity.

That distinction matters.

Because what we build without wholeness eventually demands a cost we cannot afford.

After years of marriage, motherhood, illness, leadership, and spiritual refinement, I learned that God is far less interested in what a woman can produce than in who she is becoming while she produces it.

Marriage taught me covenant—not romance as culture defines it, but commitment as formation. Seasons of ease gave way to seasons of endurance, humility, and growth. Staying was never about tolerating harm; it was about honoring God while confronting ourselves. Covenant required maturity, not illusion.

Motherhood refined me further. It demanded presence when I was depleted and integrity when convenience tempted me to disengage. My children did not need perfection—they needed a healed version of their mother. One willing to take responsibility for her inner world so they can inherit freedom, not fracture.

Professionally, I learned to lead myself before leading others. To choose excellence without applause. To refine character alongside competence. Long before I coached women, I applied the work privately—healing, unlearning, rebuilding, and aligning my life with truth.

And it was in that season—when the internal work was no longer optional—that God spoke clearly:

"You have become. Now create space for My daughters to do the same."

That is where Wife Builders was truly born.

Not as instruction—but as *discipleship*.

Not as a promise of marriage—but as a pathway to wholeness.

Not as an answer factory—but as a formation house.

The Becoming Her Council™ exists because identity must come before assignment.

Layer One—***Becoming Her***—is where the work begins. Here, women are invited to slow down, heal, and return to truth. This stage is not about outcomes; it is about alignment. It is where faith is internalized, identity is restored, and self-abandonment ends.

Layer Two—***Building Her***—follows only after foundation is laid. This is where structure, discipline, leadership, and stewardship are introduced. A woman cannot build wisely until she is rooted securely.

Layer Three—***The Inner Circle***—is reserved for women who have demonstrated readiness. This is not exclusivity for prestige, but for protection. Some rooms require discernment, maturity, and responsibility.

This is the order. And order matters.

Wife Builders does not prepare women *for marriage*—
it prepares women *for obedience.*

It is not about creating ideal wives, mothers, or leaders.
It is about forming women who are whole enough to submit to God, steward relationships with wisdom, and live from truth rather than trauma.

I do not stand as a woman who has arrived.

I stand as one who surrendered to the process.

Not as a wife who perfected covenant,
but as a woman who allowed God to mature her within it.

Not as a mother without regret,
but as one who healed forward.

Not as a coach who sells aspiration,
but as a disciple who lives in alignment.

Wife Builders is not a movement of urgency.
It is a ministry of formation.

If you are reading this, perhaps you feel that pull—not to rush ahead, but to go inward. Not to chase outcomes, but to become grounded. Not to be fixed, but to be formed.

And perhaps God is extending the same invitation He once gave me:

"Become.
Then build.
Then steward what I place in your hands."

Reflection

Scripture — Psalm 127:1 (NIV)

"Unless the Lord builds the house, the builders labor in vain."

What endures is never rushed—and it is never self-made.
Everything I have built that still stands was first surrendered.
Not in strategy sessions. Not in public moments.
But in quiet obedience. In prayer. In yielding.

Wife Builders was not constructed through visibility—it was formed through submission.
Through listening before leading.
Through allowing God to define the architecture before laying a single stone.

Legacy becomes unshakable when God is not invited as a consultant, but honored as the Architect.

Affirmation

I am becoming a woman built by God, not driven by outcomes.
I submit my plans to heaven's order and allow obedience to shape my legacy.
What I build flows from alignment, not ambition.

Sacred Prompts

- Where is God inviting you to **build—or rebuild—with Him**, rather than for Him?
- What season of your life feels unseen or uncelebrated, yet deeply formative?
- In this season, how would you define **success that honors obedience over applause**?
- Who are you becoming in God's presence when no one is watching?
- What part of your story has matured enough to be shared—not for validation, but for healing?

Chapter 12: Becoming the Answer

"God did not waste a single tear. What once felt like survival became preparation."

For a long time, I questioned the cost of my journey.
The betrayal.
The setbacks.
The seasons where healing felt slower than pain.

What I see now is this: I was not being broken—I was being prepared.

Every loss created capacity.
Every disappointment refined discernment.
Every unanswered prayer trained me to listen instead of strive.

There came a moment when I realized I was no longer waiting to be rescued.
I had become steady. Rooted. Whole.
And from that place of wholeness, I could finally serve without bleeding.

Wife Builders did not emerge from ambition—it emerged from formation.

From living the work before leading the work.
From choosing healing over hardness and obedience over image.

I no longer lead women from wounds.
I lead from wisdom.
From a life rebuilt with God as the Architect.

This is what becoming looks like:
You stop asking *why it happened* and start asking *who you are now because of it.*

And when you do, you realize—you are not behind.
You are ready.

Reflection

Isaiah 61:3 (NLT)

"...He will give a crown of beauty for ashes."

What God restores, He also repurposes.
Your healing is not just personal—it is generational.

Affirmation

I am not broken—I am built.
I lead from wholeness, serve from overflow, and walk in obedience.
What God healed in me now bears fruit through me.

Sacred Prompts

- What experiences have refined you rather than ruined you?
- Where is God inviting you to lead from wisdom instead of pain?
- What does it look like to live healed—not just hopeful?

Chapter 13: The Birth of a Movement

"What began as private healing became public fruit."

Wife Builders was never an idea—it was a response.

A response to women who loved God but had lost themselves.
Who were faithful yet fatigued.
Capable yet disconnected from their own worth.

I recognized her because I had been her.

And healing changed my vision.
I could see her clearly—not as a problem to fix, but a woman to form.

This work was never about preparing women for men.
It has always been about preparing women for covenant.
For stewardship.
For wholeness.

Wife Builders became a table—not a stage.
A place where women could become before they

perform.
Where healing came before outcomes.
Where identity preceded assignment.

This is not content.
This is cultivation.

A movement does not begin when people follow you.
It begins when people are formed.

And this one is just beginning.

Reflection

Ephesians 2:10 (NIV)

"For we are God's handiwork..."

God does not waste stories.
He shapes them into pathways for others.

Affirmation

I am formed by God and sent with purpose.
My healing serves a greater work.
I build what lasts.

Sacred Prompts

- Who is the woman you once needed?
- How is your healing preparing you to serve?
- What are you being called to cultivate—not just create?

Chapter 14: Becoming Her Was the Assignment

"Before becoming anything else, I became aligned."

Becoming Her was never about relationships.
It was about reconciliation—with myself and with God.

Healing happened slowly. Quietly. Faithfully.
In choices no one applauded.
In obedience no one saw.

I became her by choosing integrity over attention.
Stillness over striving.
Formation over performance.

Her is not an aesthetic.
She is a posture.

Whole.
Rooted.
Secure.

Wife Builders exists to protect this truth:
Marriage is a blessing—but it is not identity.

Calling precedes covenant.
Wholeness comes first.

I became her before I became his.
And that order changed everything.

Reflection

Proverbs 31:25 (NIV)

"She is clothed with strength and dignity."

Wholeness is not delayed by circumstance.
It is claimed through alignment.

Affirmation

I am whole, chosen, and aligned.
I walk in purpose—ring or not.
I am becoming exactly who God intended.

Sacred Prompts

- Where have you already grown more than you realize?
- What truth about yourself are you learning to accept?
- How can your becoming bless others?

Chapter 15: The Woman God Built

"Obedience carried me when strength ran out."

There were seasons when quitting would have made sense.

Not the dramatic kind of quitting that looks like collapse — but the quiet kind.
The kind where you stop believing for more.
The kind where you settle internally long before you settle outwardly.
The kind where you keep functioning, but you stop hoping.

Those were the moments I was tempted to lay down the work — not because I didn't love God, but because I was tired of trusting Him without evidence. Tired of believing without relief. Tired of doing the right thing while watching others take shortcuts and still prosper.

Strength wasn't what carried me through those seasons.
Obedience did.

Obedience when I didn't feel spiritual.
Obedience when my body was weak.
Obedience when my heart was disappointed.
Obedience when healing felt slower than pain.

I healed anyway.

Not instantly.
Not neatly.
But honestly.

I chose to sit with my wounds instead of numbing them.
To confront patterns instead of spiritualizing them.
To forgive where it hurt and to release what no longer had permission to live in me.

I trusted anyway.

Even when trusting again felt irresponsible.
Even when faith felt fragile.
Even when the safest thing would have been to stay guarded and self-sufficient.

Trust didn't mean ignoring wisdom — it meant refusing to let fear become my authority.

I became anyway.

I became when I wasn't applauded.
I became when progress felt invisible.
I became when growth required shedding versions of myself I once needed to survive.

This journey was never about perfection.
It was about faithfulness in becoming.

There were days I showed up unsure.
Days I prayed tired prayers.
Days I moved forward without confidence, but with conviction.

And looking back now, I can see what I couldn't see then:

God was restoring what the world had counted out — not by rushing me forward, but by rooting me deeper.

He didn't just restore opportunities.
He restored discernment.
He didn't just restore relationships.
He restored self-trust.
He didn't just restore momentum.
He restored peace.

I am not who I was — and I don't need to be.

Because the woman who stands here now is not defined by what she survived, but by what she stewarded on the other side of survival.

If my life proves anything, it's this:

You can begin again without erasing your past.
You can heal fully without pretending it didn't hurt.
You can become whole without becoming hard.

Obedience will ask more of you than strength ever could —
but it will carry you farther than strength ever will.

And if you're reading this in a season where everything in you wants to stop, slow down, or settle — hear me clearly:

You don't need more motivation.
You don't need more validation.
You don't even need more clarity.

You need permission to keep becoming — even when it's uncomfortable.

I did it anyway.

And so can you.

Reflection

Isaiah 61:3 (NIV)

"...to bestow on them a crown of beauty instead of ashes, the oil of joy instead of mourning, and a garment of praise instead of a spirit of despair."

God does not rush restoration — He completes it. What He heals, He also redeems. What He redeems, He entrusts back to you with wisdom.

Affirmation

I am a testimony in motion.
Obedience has shaped me where strength could not.
I am healed, whole, I AM THE BLUEPRINT.

Sacred Prompts

Sit with these questions gently. Let honesty lead.

- Where have you continued forward even when quitting felt justified?
- What version of yourself did you have to release in order to heal?
- How has obedience carried you when confidence could not?
- What does "becoming anyway" look like in this current season?
- Who are you now that survival is no longer your identity?

Chapter 16: From Survival to Strategy

"Wholeness brings clarity. Clarity brings direction."

Survival reacts.
Strategy responds.

When I stopped living in crisis mode, I could finally hear God clearly.
And clarity changed everything.

Strategy did not mean striving—it meant stewardship.
Of my time.
My energy.
My calling.

I built boundaries that protected peace.
Rhythms that honored rest.
A life aligned with who I was becoming.

This is not a glow-up.
This is formation.

You were not created to survive your life.
You were created to steward it.

And now, you can.

Closing Truth

Becoming Her is not a destination.
It is a way of living.

And if you've made it here—
You're already on the path.

A Letter to the Woman Still Becoming

Hun,

If you made it to this page, then you already know: You are not broken. You are becoming.

I wrote this book with trembling fingers and a bold heart. Not for applause. Not for pity. But for you. For the woman who has cried on bathroom floors, smiled through betrayal, and prayed herself back to life.

You are not alone.

Every chapter of my story was a brick. Some were jagged with pain. Others were soaked in faith. But I laid them down, one by one, and built a life I no longer needed to escape from.

And you can too.

Maybe you've been silenced by shame. Maybe you've been stuck in survival mode. But hear me when I say this: There is still time to become the woman God intended. You don't need permission to heal. You need conviction.

Choose yourself. Trust God. Do the work. And never forget that becoming her starts with a single, sacred yes.

I believe in you. I see you. I am you.

With love and fire,

Donniseca

Letter to 18-Year-Old Me

Dear Donniseca,

You are not crazy for dreaming bigger than your environment. You are not selfish for wanting something different. And you are not weak because you're tired. You are just 18, standing at the edge of a life no one prepared you for.

You are about to face decisions that will crack you wide open—but those cracks will become highways for God's glory. You think love is supposed to hurt, but it isn't. You think you have to prove your worth to be chosen, but you don't.

One day, you will rise. You will walk out of brokenness carrying purpose in your hands. You will become the woman you're praying to meet right now.

Stay tender, stay teachable, and never stop talking to God.

Love,

The Woman You've Become

Letter to My Baby Girl

My Dearest Kay Girl,

You are not just my daughter. You are God's masterpiece. Fearfully and wonderfully made. Born for impact, not approval.

Right now, you are learning who you are, and it may feel heavy. You give too much. You silence your voice. You shrink when you were built to shine. But hear your mama clearly: you are more than enough.

You don't have to earn love by pleasing people. The right people will love you simply because you are YOU. You don't have to dim your brilliance to make others comfortable. You don't have to carry everyone to feel worthy.

You were never meant to be invisible.

God has plans for you that go beyond what you see today. You are becoming the woman this world needs. A woman who walks in truth, power, and peace. Let God grow you. Let life refine you. And let your worth be rooted in the One who created you.

Because Kay Girl... you are the promise.

Love always,

Mom

Letter to Myself after Divorce

Hun,

I know your heart is in pieces, but hear me when I say this with all the authority God gave me: you are not broken—you are being rebuilt.

You stood in that apartment, over drafted, exhausted, and numb. The silence screamed louder than any goodbye ever could. And even though he left in the middle of the night like a coward—you woke up that morning whole.

You didn't feel whole.

You felt like a failure.

You replayed every argument, every second-guess, every red flag you tried to bleach white. You kept thinking, "How did I get here?"

But baby, you didn't get there because you were weak—you got there because you were strong enough to try. Over and over again.

You fought for your marriage. You carried his weight, his laziness, his lies, and still showed up for your kids and your career like a boss. And when your body couldn't take it anymore? When your blood sugar dropped and you nearly lost your life?

You still didn't quit. You still gave him another chance. And he still chose betrayal.

So, let's settle this now:

You were never the problem.

His neglect doesn't make you unlovable.

His cheating doesn't make you undesirable.

His leaving doesn't make you forgettable.

What it does make you—is free.

You are free now to feel your feelings without fear.

Free to breathe without bracing for disappointment.

Free to be loved the way God designed—from the crown on your head to the cracks in your heart.

You chose you.

And that was the first righteous decision in a long time.

Hold your head high, Miss Dillon. This ain't the end of your story—it's the part where your power starts talking back.

A Letter to My Love, Jason

Jason My Love,

There are no words big enough to hold the kind of gratitude I carry for you—but I'm going to try.

You came into my life when the storm had nearly swallowed me whole. I had walked through betrayal, abandonment, and survival-mode motherhood. I was bruised in places no one could see—and still, you saw me. You didn't flinch. You didn't run. You stood still... and chose me.

You loved the whole me—my healed parts and my healing ones. You never asked me to shrink. You never made me feel like I had to perform. You didn't try to fix me. You simply held space for me. And that, my love, healed me.

The love I see in your eyes—it's steady. It's warm. It's the kind of love that doesn't rush in and out with convenience, but abides. You give me safety, not just protection. You offer peace, not just provision. You bring joy, not just jokes. And the way you see me? It makes me want to be softer, fuller, and more me every single day.

You are the gift I didn't even know I was allowed to pray for. God must've spent extra time crafting your heart to match mine. You were made for me... and I for you.

Thank you for loving my children like they are your own.

Thank you for loving me when I'm loud and when I'm quiet.

Thank you for choosing us—every day.

We've had our rough spots, sure. But the beauty is that we never stopped choosing. And that's what makes our love different. It's not fantasy—it's covenant. It's not just romance—it's real.

I am honored to be your wife.

I am grateful to grow beside you.

And I will spend the rest of my days loving you back—with my whole, healed, and becoming heart.

Forever Yours,

Donniseca

Letter to Becoming Her: The Woman You Are Now

Hey Beautiful,

Look at you.

No, really—look at you.

You are the woman you prayed to become. You're not perfect, but you are whole. You've been shattered and reshaped. Betrayed and still built better. You've survived things that tried to bury you, and now you walk in rooms carrying light they can't quite name.

You are her.

Not because of the titles or the testimonials. Not because of your marriage, your motherhood, or your milestones. But because you did the work. You got on your knees when it didn't make sense. You faced the mirror and finally told the truth. You held space for your healing and still showed up for others with soft hands and a sharp spirit.

You love God out loud now.

You honor your body, protect your peace, and guard your name with wisdom and fire.

You walk in purpose and let your "no" be holy and your "yes" be strategic.

You are the blueprint now.

The girl who once begged for crumbs now sets full tables. The woman who once questioned her worth now teaches others how to find their own. You didn't just bounce back—you broke cycles.

Every scar you carry is now oil in your anointing.

Every 'no' you endured created space for this divine yes.

And even now, as you continue becoming, you do it without apology.

You are not waiting for approval.

You are not asking for permission.

You are aligned. Anointed. And unshakable.

This season? It belongs to you. And so does the next.

Keep becoming. Keep building. Keep shining.

With reverence and pride,

Donniseca

Final Encouragements & Conclusion: The Woman God is Building

Hun, if you've made it this far, then you've walked every step of this journey with me. And I pray you felt seen. Not just in my struggle—but in your own becoming.

You now know I didn't get here in stilettos and sequins. I crawled through heartbreak. I bled through betrayal. I limped through disappointment. But I didn't stop. I couldn't.

I kept becoming.

I kept believing.

I kept building.

And now here I am, telling you: You can too.

This isn't just a memoir. It's a mirror. A mirror for every woman who's ever asked herself:

Am I too broken to be loved?

Is this all life has for me?

Can anything good come from this pain?

Hun,

You are not too far gone.

You are not too messed up.

And no matter what they said, what they did, or what you believed—your story doesn't end with survival.

It begins with strategy.

You're not just a product of what happened to you. You're the producer of what's next. Let that settle in your spirit.

If I Could Leave You with 5 Final Reminders:

- You are not what you've been through. You are who God says you are—whole, worthy, chosen.
- Closure is not required for you to heal. Sometimes the only apology you'll get is your own decision to move on.
- Love isn't supposed to hurt. If it breaks your spirit more than it builds your soul, it's not love—it's bondage.
- Trust the pace of your own unfolding.
- Joy is your birthright. Don't let pain evict it. Reclaim it daily.

And to every woman who thought she wouldn't make it...

Let this book be proof that you can rebuild.

Let it be your permission slip to leave what no longer serves you.

Let it be the fire under your dreams, the balm for your wounds, and the anthem in your ear when the nights get heavy.

Because here's the truth: I didn't wait for the perfect timing. I didn't have a fairy tale blueprint. I didn't even have consistent support.

But I had God.

And I had grit.

And I had the audacity to believe that there was more for me—even when my circumstances whispered "settle."

So, if you're still sitting in your brokenness, sis... stand up.

If you've been waiting on a sign... this is it.

And if you don't feel ready, let me say what nobody said to me back then:

You were never meant to stay broken.

You were built to bloom.

So, cry if you need to. Shout if you must. But then—dry your tears, fix your crown, and walk in your becoming.

You don't need anyone's permission.

You already have mine.

And more importantly, you have God's.

I love you. I'm rooting for you. And I promise—

If I did it anyway... you can too.

Behind the Pages: Author's Note

The Story Behind “I Did It Anyway: The Woman Who Chose Herself and Lived to Tell It”

I didn’t write this book for applause. I wrote it because I survived.

I wrote it because too many women are still silencing their pain with polite smiles and “I’m fine's while bleeding out behind closed doors. I wrote it because I remember the days when I couldn’t see past my next heartbreak, my next unpaid bill, my next mistake. I wrote it for the woman who’s doing her best and still feeling like it’s not enough. Sis, I see you—because I was you.

This book started as a whisper in my soul—a divine nudge that wouldn’t let me rest until I answered. For years, I carried my story like luggage I was too afraid to unpack. It was heavy, but familiar. Painful, but protective. I told myself that parts of my story were too messy, too personal, too embarrassing to share. But then God reminded me that healing doesn’t happen in hiding. It happens in the light.

Writing I Did It Anyway wasn’t therapeutic—it was surgical. I had to cut deep. I had to revisit wounds I thought were already healed. I had to call things what they really were: betrayal, abandonment, emotional abuse, survival, resilience, grace. I had to look at the girl I used to be—the one who cried herself to sleep with a baby on her hip and a prayer in her throat—and I had to love her enough to tell her truth.

So why now? Why this book?

Because I’m living proof that choosing yourself isn't selfish—it’s sacred.

I spent years putting everyone else’s needs ahead of my own. I stayed in relationships that chipped away at my self-worth, convincing myself I had to settle to be loved. I kept trying to earn love I never had to audition for in the first place. And when it all fell apart—when I found myself broke, broken, and barely breathing—I had to ask one life-changing question:

What if I choose me this time?

That question changed everything. It didn’t fix my life overnight, but it put me on the path to healing, wholeness, and the kind of love story I never thought I deserved—first with myself, and eventually with Jason, the man God handcrafted just for me.

This book is for the woman who's made mistakes. The woman who stayed too long. The one who thought she could love him enough to fix it. The one who's raising babies, building a career, healing from church hurt, hiding her tears in bathroom stalls at work, and still showing up. Sis, you're doing better than you think. And this book is a mirror to remind you of who you are—and who you're becoming.

Yes, I talk about the ugly stuff.

The infidelity. The betrayal. The silence.

The morning, I couldn't wake up and my children were crying beside my bed.

The time I moved across states with a toddler, a pre-teen, a tank full of gas, and not a single dollar to waste.

But I also talk about redemption.

About finding my voice.

About rebuilding my life from the ground up with God's grace and a whole lot of grit.

About motherhood, entrepreneurship, second chances, and the kind of love that doesn't just whisper "I choose you," but shows up for it—daily.

This book birthed Wife Builders—my calling, my coaching, my movement. It's more than a brand. It’s a blueprint for every woman who refuses to settle for dysfunction disguised as destiny. Through this story, I wanted to leave behind more than memories. I wanted to leave a map.

Because every healed woman becomes a lighthouse for the one still searching in the dark.

And if my pain can become someone else's permission to heal, then it was all worth it.

So here it is: the raw, uncut, faith-fueled truth of how I lost myself, found God, and became the woman I was always destined to be.

I did it anyway.

And Sis... so can you.

With love and holy boldness,

Donniseca West

Book Club & Personal Sacred Questions

Which chapter impacted you the most, and why?

What moment in the book made you feel seen?

What lesson are you taking with you from Donniseca's story?

Who do you need to forgive to move forward?

What does "choosing yourself" look like in this season of your life?

Where are you still becoming her?

What would you tell the version of you from 5 years ago?

How has this book changed the way you view relationships?

What promise are you still holding on to?

What will your "The Woman God Built" story be?

Ready to keep becoming her?

Visit my website: donnisecadwest.com

More Books by Donniseca

Becoming the Blueprint

She Is Becoming

www.ingramcontent.com/pod-product-compliance
Lightning Source LLC
LaVergne TN
LVHW010937110826
845149LV00013B/2642

* 9 7 9 8 9 9 4 0 7 2 3 9 4 *